INVENTION

INVENTION

by
ANNE WALDMAN
and
SUSAN HALL

THE KULCHUR FOUNDATION

Edited by Lita Hornick
Design by Lita Hornick
INVENTION
by Anne Waldman & Susan Hall
Copyright © 1985 by Anne Waldman & Susan Hall
Published by The Kulchur Foundation
888 Park Ave., N.Y., N.Y. 10021
Library of Congress Cataloging in Publication Data
Waldman, Anne, 1945–
  Invention.

  Poems by A. Waldman; drawings by S. Hall.
  I. Hall, Susan, 1943–   II. Title.
PS3573.A4215I5 1985   811'.54   85–57
ISBN 0–936538–09–0 (pbk.)

    Printed in the U.S.A. by Capital City Press
          Montpelier, Vermont

CONTENTS

"What is she doing?" Sophie asked Mary.

"A dance to the sun, I think," Sophie said.
"She told me to sit here and watch her."

— Jane Bowles,
TWO SERIOUS LADIES

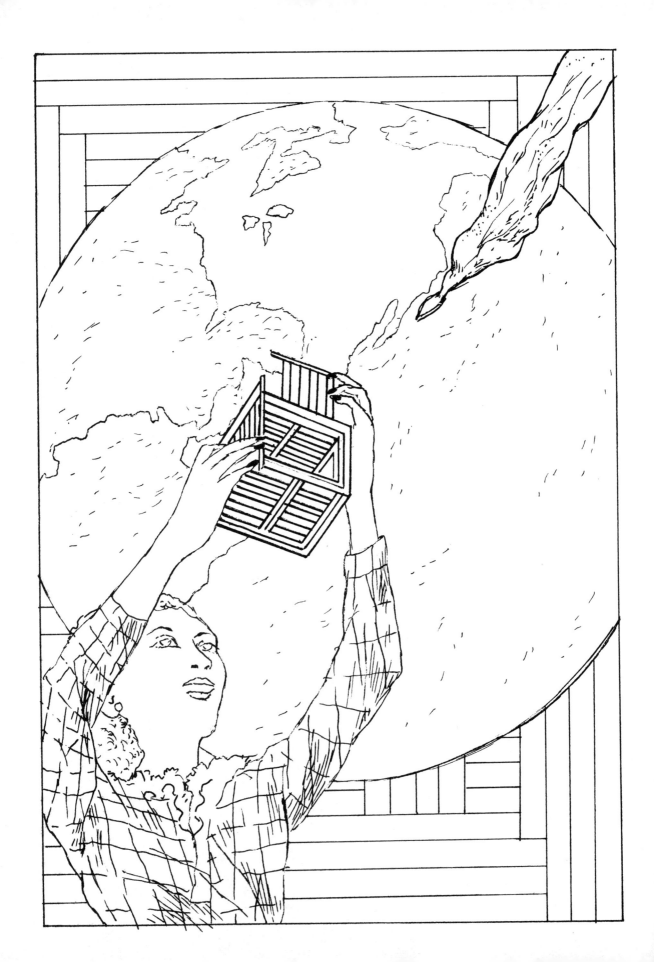

On Walt Whitman's Birthday

O strategic map of disasters, hungry America
O target for the song, the jouncing poem,
the protest
A long imperfect history shadows you
Let all suffering, toil, sex &
sublime distractions go unrecorded
Let the world continue to breathe

It's simple: a woman gets up & stretches
The world is her mirror & portal too

(Whitmanic morning task: waken the country to itself)

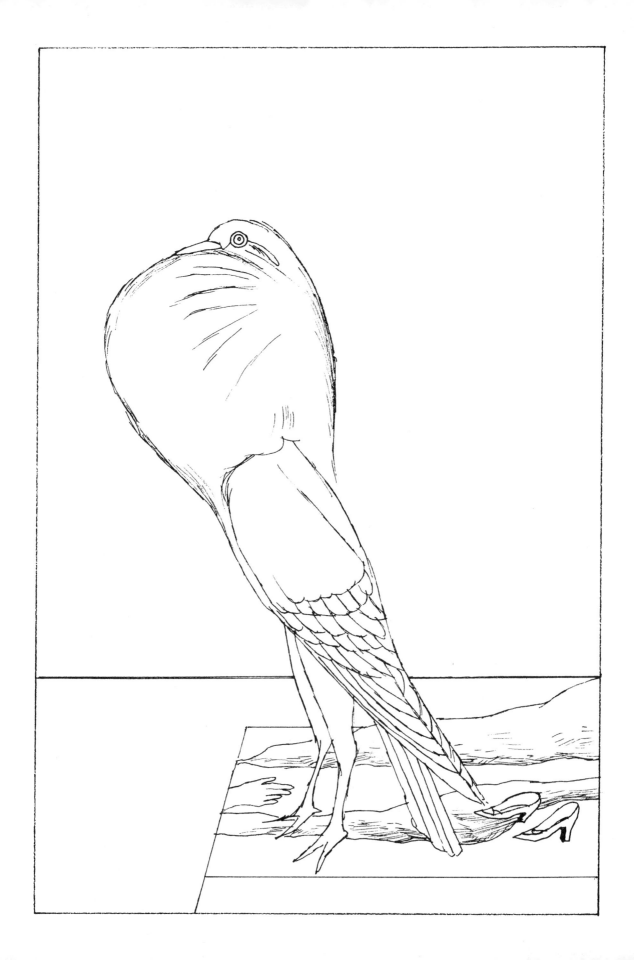

Diva

She never lost her voice or pounds
She sang "You pen the door, girls, but
    don't box me in!"
She had her fans
The girls go backstage with their pens

Opera buffs go mad for this sort of day
waiting in line under puffy trees in San Francisco

A strong lung puffs up passion
& theatrically steps out into the light

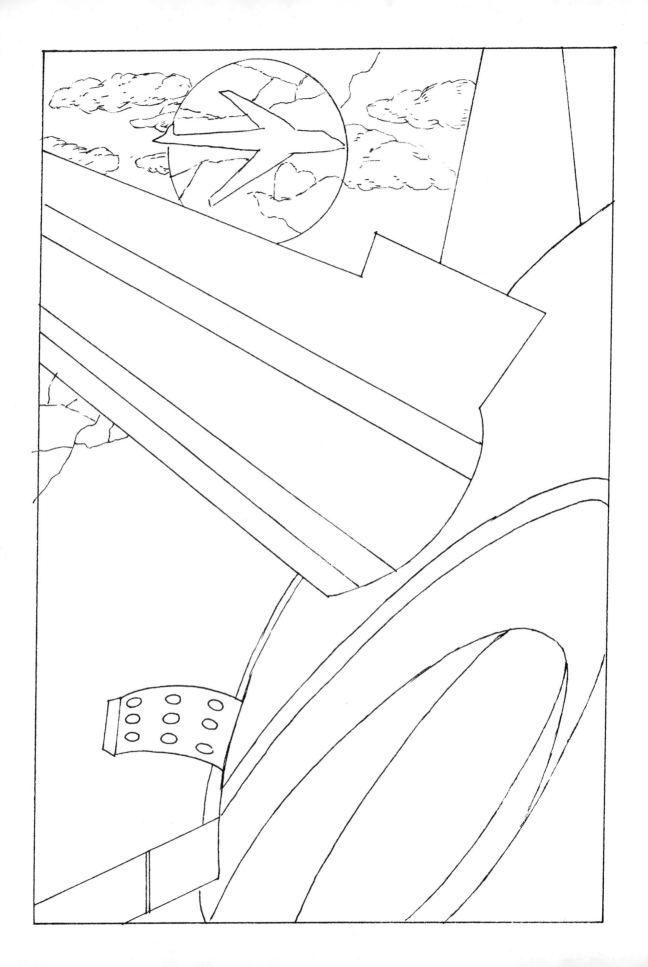

Miles Above

To be silent was a thought concerning you
who are spending long periods of time
hermetically sealed
You know, I just arrived the spine a burning
question: is sex securely fastened?

The stewardess has poisoned me out of jealousy
She knows your naked trunk is curvaceous
"But relax, have another"

I've resolved recalcitrantly on suing
your impressario
He's strewn with too many engagements
& bookkeepers now, his memory's running away

I'm running away to die in Reno
Think of me whose shaking hand wrote
these lines light years above your heart

Bijou

Marlene gets her dots off the Borneo maps

Her armadillo metallic travelling dress shudders

She was once singing as the Everyboy Navy, eyebrows
    painted above the horizon of her face

Marlene sashays up the gangplank like an imploded sex device

A deserting sailor acts as bouncer

She also has a pickpocket up her sleeve with eyes
    like Gurdjieff

Men pop hot muscles & fall over each other

This could never happen in Kansas City, Kansas

Last frame: she lets seedy doctor, hurt by life,
    buy her a drink.

People Are Seen By Animals

Happy cat would love to jump off
your love of steak & water
Everything & the naugahyde cushions must go
Tame you in a cage, wild people
Put you many times in a box, people
Your human voices grate like stone on metal
Satie at the piano doing no better
Alligators don't dream & function ruthlessly
to grow back a limb
The radar of bats is superior
to all your instruments
There's a tinge of condescension
in your biscuit, as if to say
we are easily humored
You are weird & impolite,
O politicians of D.C.!
The cat's meow is an anthem to us
It's like we're from Mars
not so smooth of skin as you are
but sexier, more circumspect,
We never smile

Bill's Old Girl

The day was on fire but the night was still young
to Bill's old girl

She was caught

Rattle your bracelets Bill's old girl

Bill's girlfriend: is she down by the lake again?

Bill's girl rode a train to get here

She was romantic about animals

Bill's girlfriend used to star gaze before she
became impatient

She always had some questions about what it meant
to be born under the sign of Pisces

She kept her admirers dangling on a line

And then there was always Bill

Ms. Stein

Ms. Stein likes it with sunlight & a kitchen
Ms. Stein lives on a street named Flowers
Ms. Stein is proud of you, Alice
All the chairs are in an arrangement
Ms. Stein, Ms. Stein your nightlamp's on!
Ms. Stein in a handsome suit with velvet trim
Head, you were a talking Buddha
She cuts down a recent visitor with a sentence
        about professionalism
I said she was a big woman: big belly,
        trunks for legs, feet on the ground
        sturdy pumps
She sits, legs apart, on a big chair
Is she walking with a cane
Holding her spine straight in Baltimore?
There was always talking & sitting
What was she thinking late at night
Was it this way to be working in Eternity
thinking: the present moment is the final reality?
She thinks: My ego's a sieve
I'm a big woman full of words

Savonarola On My Mind: A Valentine

You enter, report Now there are 3 stars in a triangle
                                over the mountain
I say Planets & yearn to go outside myself drifting
among heavenly bodies & have my heart extend as magnanimously
                                as sky
but glued instead to novel ROMOLA & Savonarola's dark fate
& that of Romola's wicked cad of a husband, not wicked
                                exactly, rather, immoral
I can't stand his good looks & suave words!

I delight in your soft-spoken words
saying How they had but pennies, showing me photos of Gaudier-
                                Brzeska cat & stone mountain
head of Ezra Pound. Now radio is telling some immoral
news, baby is snorting, & Romola is drifting
in nun's garb in a boat toward the hideous pestilence, sad fate
of 15th century humans, but she will escape. People say she is
                                angel-madonna sent from friendly sky

How different was the Florentine sky from Boulder sky?
Did the oratorical Savonarola's visions come with words?
Was it always a matter of a sealed fate,
clandestine letters intercepted, false rumor, mountains
of florins stashed away, power shifting & drifting
with the tide? Is it an immoral

proposition to found a true Republic? Immoral
in the sense of uneasiness, not uninspired. The sky's
no limit when it comes to history, and drifting
past, we too will have our words
dissolve in a rumble of taxcuts, warmongering! Modern fate
may be unkind although these mountains

aren't. They sit outside our lives with wondrous mountain
logic, won't brook no fleshy disaster, immoral
dealings, not that we must either, in fact, we won't. Our fate
was to make precious blue sky
baby eyes & never stop putting in words
the best of imagination & leave drifting

to the brook across the road. Drifting
as in a dream, drifting as in snowdrift on a mountain
side. Will there always be a Savonarola or Pound to set the words
for an era? Are we part of one too? Is this era immortal?
Questions for the vortex, more ego-centric magazines arrive,
                    tragic fire fate
announced & a new kind of panda-mouse is discovered under
                    China's sky

That mountain top is the tip of my heart. Thoughts are drifting
in February's ether. Jupiter & Saturn conjoin in Colorado
tonight. Our fate is married to this century, my love. Romola
lived in an immoral fiction, which is how I began these words.

Two American Nozzle Relics

Especially if you sing it accurately with smiles
"quando ti risponda fiocheto e piano"
(while I amuse you in Italian all weak & speaking low)
How many poets before her sang, why they sang their lives away!
Baryshnikov began with a mild flirtation
of owls & cuckoos, asses, apes & dogs
who only stand & wait to dance or drink from woodland well
like music's soft splendour, ocean's deep
But I love you Child of Quiet when we have the last dance
You say it's 11:13 & I say "no war"
I'll dance to that, but do not forget belly relics
Live, prosper, dare a final bound
I dreamed I was at a party for all the Lansing girls
They like to dance to any Motown record from 1965

A tree stump whispers me ancient messages
"It's her turn, up front", it insists
Ambitious young women & baccalaureates whose clever
shadow-families sleep by the moon prefer that
5 new tables clip this: belly relics
Who settles a private life boiling the brick
Stomped scissors & I stopped them
On a wall in a room on a Sunday afternoon: bumper crop illusion,
Wisconsin cheddar, Hawaiian punch, Louisiana hot sauce
To hold the bite of the spirits back since
conceiving of moving the rhubarb is useless
Raincoat sleeve indicates: which is a wind is not rain
or fetch me a cognac from under yon couch, please
Splashed egges, pinball machines & other street dimensions
For years a girl is rolling the carpets out to dry

Alaska Pipe Dream

Alaska pipeline
stagnant on one side
of the question
Tart words forge ahead
a government
Tribesmen sitting
or standing, asking
what about the ghosts
& wild beasts? Will
they like this?
Trenchant head
observes progress
with a head
to steam up
a battle-ax type notion
from the floor
You might reject
another head
as being out of hand
Eskimo heads
salute the man
who heads up
his ancestry
& fact of struggle
while white hands vote
to be hard of head
Steel-headed
A padded metallic glove lies in
the snow

Joanne

She suffers even in medicines, idols,
refuses cool guys though they be gallant
with all that breezing. Movements of
this kind arouse the humor of the living
lady and stress incantation over formula
and laughter's just an ornament, be it
ordinary or supreme. Finds jewels in
those whose vanity comes apart and
tolerates carelessness in a kind of
walking she does so well and bones,
nerves, organs come alive, charmed
to consider annotated pages conceived
in grace and required by a long
skill in quixotic luxury singing.

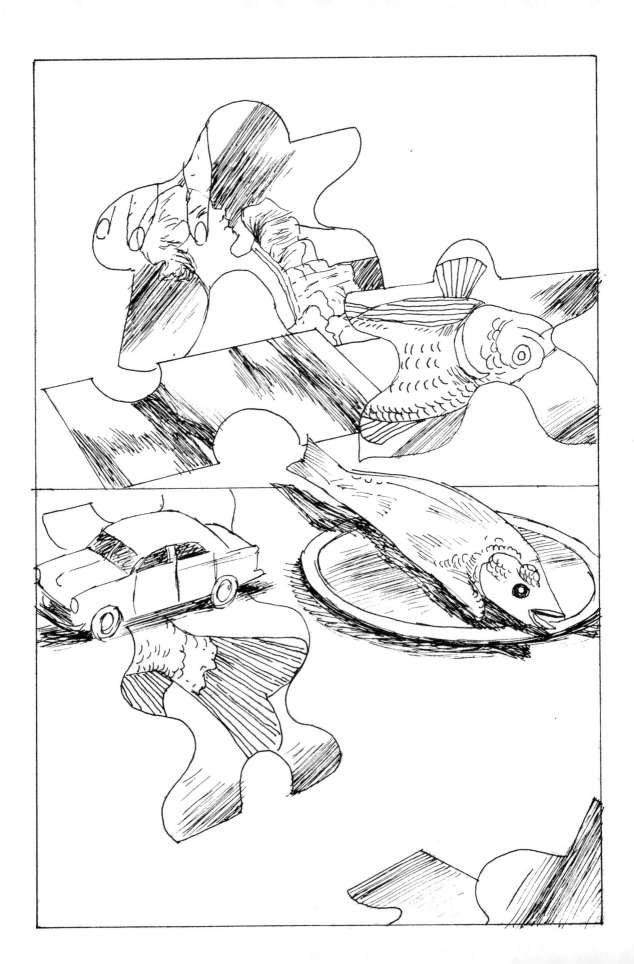

Replacement

I am watching how one is changing my place
one & one
his face lighted by relief in replacement
I am watching how he is larger than the other one
one & one & one
immense & moving
My thinking of the little boy on his face
I am watching how they are changing their faces
while mine remains the same

My thinking is not on my face
it is on my immense body
larger than ever in the big space
They are lighted by relief
to know how everything changes
the boy will change
the man will almost change
she changes every day
The other people are not standing still
but replacing each other in a little while

Colored puzzle pieces of the United States
tumble on the rug
People change their clothes & talk
The expressions on their faces are replaced by new ones
The boy picks up the blue shape landed at his feet
"Oklahoma!"

I Thought I Was In Films

A train on your thoughts, buzzard thoughts to get home on a
blizzard, taking a car in Duluth, a plane to Twin Cities, a
walk, a taxi in Washington. I got to Union Station and boarded
a Metroliner. "Not a blizzard, but a different motor assurance
needed to be. But your ticket says Philadelphia, so it's
$9.25 more." (Conductor: dark, Italian.) Four cars with designated
smoking and a parlour all scented up. Calls aboard abroad to
my family and lover. I read: Helena Morley skips in the dappled
sunlight. Colette lies abed on her 75th birthday, pained but
spry. Thank you for A BLUE LANTERN. Edwin's birthday February
5, Burroughs too, a blanket of snow, many trees, a more wooded
area, grass illuminated by sun-going-down. Plus some now
assimilated house half-lit by pulsar sun (25 minutes out of
Baltimore). I want to say it's your lips, no your hands,
elbows, no your kneecaps, no. Stop. Say hello to the guys across
the aisle discussing the "Awards". "That actress was simply
a thin one!" They seem to be "in theatre". I'm abstemious,
thank you anyway, forging to forgive the blizzard for being
my detour. Now 2 geese in tandem, more tender now more than 19
now hundreds over the big lake, Big Lake Delay. See them forget to
swirl. And a mist coming off the lake making you
think I was in films. Icing everywhere
and someone, a girl-woman, is walking out on a pair of legs on
a mink pier. One appears to like her, following after.
Does my mind not appear to be on my work? More overheard
conversation: "Should we put antlers on the wheelchair?"
"Let's talk about how Robbie is dressed in this scene." "I'll
probably use the nurse as a doctor." "Several weeks later,
during the day, she's lost in Pocatello. Don't forget she's
a very strange combination of woman and girl." "Ok, who
else is in this scene?" "Maybe she could be wearing a white
overcoat! And he'd be in maroon pajamas decorated with little
turquoise horseshoes. Things have happened to them socially,
know what I mean?"

"Let me guide your coat to the overhead rack."

A Phone Call From Frank O'Hara
"That all these dyings may be life in death"

I was living in San Francisco
My heart was in Manhattan
It made no sense, no reference point
Hearing the sad horns at night,
fragile evocations of female stuff
The 3 tones (the last most resonant)
were like warnings, haiku-muezzins at dawn
The call came in the afternoon
"Frank, is that really you?"
I'd awake chilled at dawn
in the wooden house like an old ship
Stay bundled through the day
sitting on the stoop to catch the sun
I lived near the park whose deep green
over my shoulder made life cooler
Was my spirit faltering, grown duller?
I want to be free of poetry's ornaments,
its duty, free of constant irritation,
me in *it*, what was grander reason
for being? Do it, why? (Why, Frank?)
To make the energies dance etc.
My coat a cape of horrors
I'd walk through town of
impending earthquake. Was that it?
Ominous days. Street shiny with
hallucinatory light on sad dogs,
too many religious people, or a woman
startled me by her look of indecision
near the empty stadium
I walked back spooked by
my own darkness
Then Frank called to say
"What? Not done complaining yet?
Can't you smell the eucalyptus,
have you never neared the Pacific?
'While frank and free/ Call for
musick while your veins swell'"
he sang, quoting a metaphysician

"Don't you know the secret, how to
wake up and see you don't exist, but
that does, don't you see phenomena
is so much more important than *this*?
I always love *that*."
"Always?" I cried, wanting to believe him
"Yes". "But say more! How *can* you if
it's sad & dead?" "But that's just it!
If! It isn't. *It* doesn't want to be
Do *you* want to be?" He was warming to his song:
"Of course I don't have to put up with as
much as you do these days. These *years*.
But I do miss the color, the architecture,
the talk. You know, it *was* the life!
And dying is such an insult. After all
I was in love with breath and I loved
embracing those others, the lovers
with my *body*." He sighed & laughed
He wasn't quite as I'd remembered him
Not less generous, but more abstract
Did he even have a voice now, I wondered
or did I think it up in the middle
of this long day, phone in hand now
dialing Manhattan

Posse

We have a posse of women
patrolling the canyon

Rachel The Regenerative

Claudia The Able-Bodied

Denyse of Dense Desire

Melinda darted here from Michigan

Simone-Near-Utah never slumbers

This is the humblest Top of the Susans!
next to Canadian Sarah
while Floridian Cindy wields the scissors

When Taking-Liberties comes up
WE CRUSH HIM DOWN!

July 4th

Wood green. Grandfather built it.
But Grandfather is dead. He puts
down the glassblower's tube to die
a Lutheran. He starts the black
Ford sedan one last time. He wears
working glass spectacles on his
pale face.

Metal holders are spread like
fans on the front of the house
supporting American flags small enough
a child can wave as the boats go by.

Karyogamy

The gardener works on the tent pole
Lines move beyond the plot he tends
off to one side in Providence
Now he sets up a tent for a wedding
It's raining. The bride is depressed
She passes the gardener who reeks of magnolia
by the bubbling fountain
She's not seen
She stuffs a blue item in her bra
She already made love to this groom months ago
No one wants to feel restraint
Why does the gardener hide in the cellar?
Where is her restraint?
Why should she orbit about this husband to be
she asks
A plot he intends to instigate in how
he'll (the gardener) rule their lives
is worrisome to M L & J
One family member cares a lot
An uncle like a mannikin blows smoke in the air
Cough cough
Unguarded moment of a wet day leads nowhere really
Why worry? What day is it?
Hers, and it's coming for her

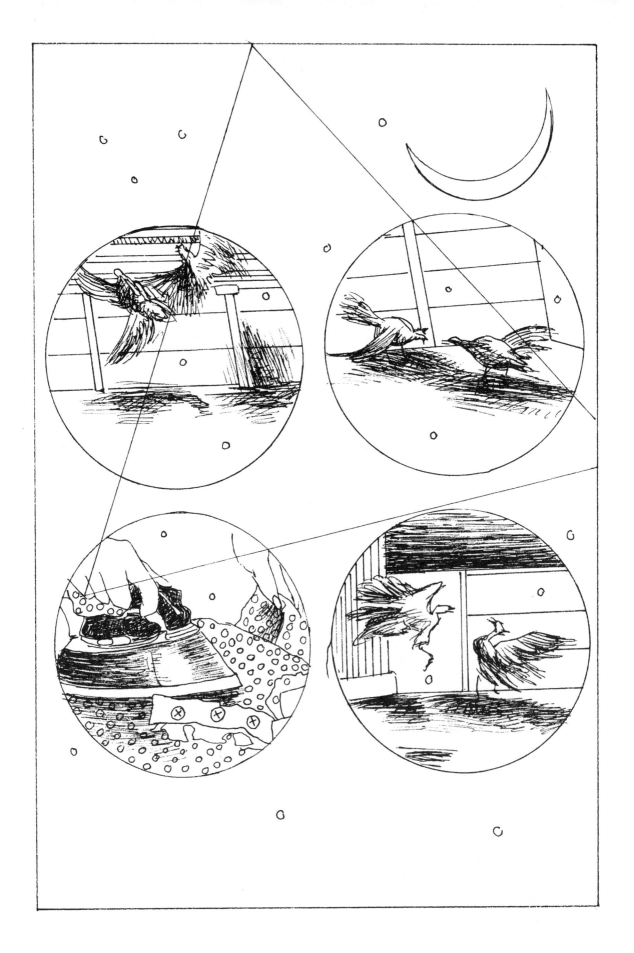

Triangle

The 2nd moon curled in a grimace
Sandy's lips parted to sing
      "If only the animal could find its way . . ."
This was Iowa, a song of vivacity

If only to give each other a boost
the town boasted thousands remote
to make up for its distance from the rest of us

Is a town like a faithless husband?
Is it underdressed as usual?
Or is it undressed like a woman
standing before her bath
passed down, the bathtub that is,
a few generations

The woman murmurs
"Al-dhanab al-asad, the lion's tail!
With Arcturus and Spica, Denebola forms
      an equilateral triangle!"

Sandy takes care of two
and divides her energy three ways
She gazes at the stars humming as she works

This was one's friends in Iowa,
a song of perspicacity

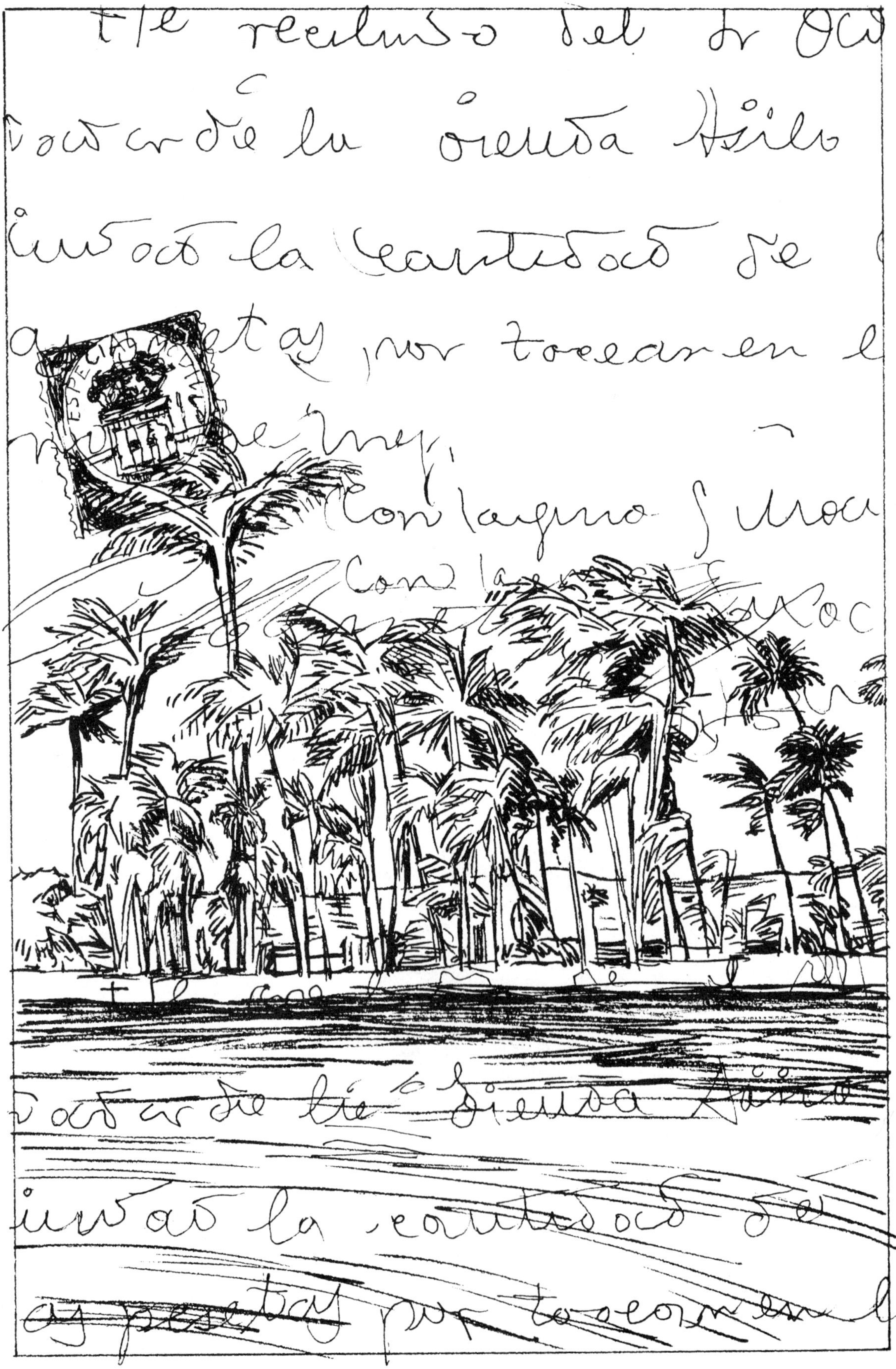

Florida Music

Palm talk? We are those
succulent & shiny (green) leaves
Could a figure in all this who made you
laugh grow up & ever move away?
She was a flower too
tended in the expensive people's garden
A life starts from seed
She was costly, arrayed like a hybrid princess
Stick your nose up in Florida & float
The sea is a difficult neighbor
& flows over you mercilessly & you reminisce
You are groomed to be topical
coming down the stair, cocktail in hand
You will be blown & tossed by wind,
a scattered bounty

Aristocracy Of The Brain

put in "the divine magnet is on you & the magnet responds"
put in the aristocracy of the brain
put in a good story: the earth is smeared with scented water
put in the lesser vehicle
put in "don't need no cayenne pepper!"
put in the Fear Survey: 25% of Americans afraid to go outside
                         6% afraid of someone breaking into their
                         homes
put in strong-arm hedonism
put in a tall bare torso
take out radar
Call Approach 25 zero Roger
put in "Cricket Lifting Tongs of Carved Tortoise Shell"
put in slices of cowhorn worked with diligent fingers
put in Fantastic Weathered Rock
put in The Paradise of Tejaprabha Buddha Attended by Sun Moon
      Stars & Five Planets as Deities (Tempera on clay 13th Cent.)
put in her frail constitution upside down
put in lusty guys doing the drunk dance
put in a mad scene where she dies of a broken heart
put in the barren steppes of Anatolia
put in the Sacred Toad Ashram
put in the black marble vase from Peking Bookstore, St. Louis
put in a poem to the Madonna
put in just a string of wooden beads
put in "for me, it's become sorta a bird"
put in a local relic fossil outside Cheyenne
notice how the canvas wears whenever the sun's in my eyes

Alice Aurora

Alice aurora
Alice andante
Alice auspicious
Alice aviary
Alice autocracy
Alice availing
Alice in azure
Alice callous
Alice à ciel
Alice airy
Alice allay my fears
Alice albacore
Alice arboreal
An allegory is elucidated
almanac Alice
Alice glue down
Alice Alonzo Stagg
Alice ababa
Alice ambivalent
Anthropocentric Alice
Alice Altair
Amenable Alice
Anomaly, Alice
Adagio Alice
Ablative Absolute
Absolutely, Alice
Alice gladly
Alice of Arizona
Alicia Alimentaria
appreciate this Alice

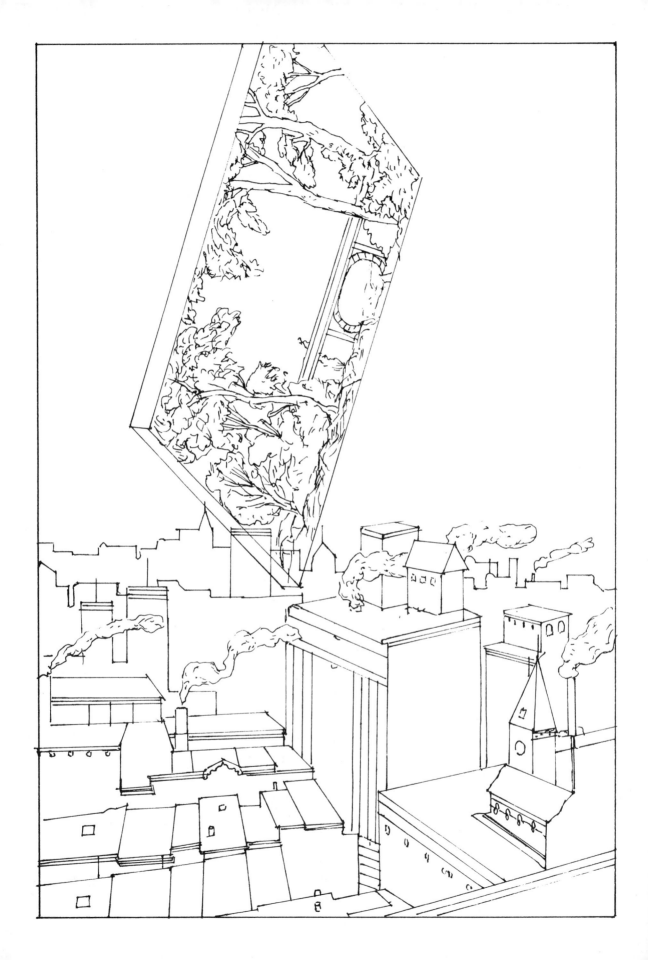

Penelope's Version

In a minute: daniel cell, magnets, iron fillings
In an hour: tangent galvanometer
In a day: asunder
In an epoch: people tormented by doubt: environment

    & in a city & wooed by a city & in a city
    not a home city but a city in which things
    could be made cunningly

    (intricate search for what I know in architecture
    say in Atlanta, Georgia), Penelope said

Let's put an illusion or movement or actually
a bridge, a park, anti-pavement, where it isn't
designed
       & a space for mothers
Penelope said (she was pregnant then) This is important

As A Black Man Moves

A most astonishing thing is moving
as a black man moves under clothes

He was not thinking of this
but thinking: rooms
He was in Alabama rooms

"Are you whose arrival portends
riches?"
he asked
"I've gotten stuck twice & disappeared"

"In one year I've shouted all my songs
as if music was shook down
like apples from a tree"

He was outside now
Not thinking: rooms

He was sweating as he turned
to the man, smiling & lifting the guitar
as the man turned on the tape recorder

Alabama, a little time ago
moving like a river under clothes

"Walk on Roses"

Melodrama of someone's youth
A silent film in which mouths are moving
A piano pumping the action up
Someone cuts across a wide street
And someone weeps
in what could be Connecticut
because it is seen like a dream: still, contained
Someone is younger than you'll ever be
& someone coughs bending down to retrieve
a candy wrapper depicting a girl with a big red sash
In the same movie theatre a cartoon mouse
with top hat is featured
This mouse has been romping in a lot
of film houses lately as have
the newsreels of the Great War
and the times before, & before that
A newscaster's voice is tense
with the details of that fighting day
The day is swallowed up again
More pennies are spent at the concession out front
A couple is quarreling in the back row
The girl on the screen makes a concession
to her darkhaired lover and the movie ends
on a petulant kiss

The Rebuilding Of Detroit

Once upon a time a person became more than one of us,
etched in a smile. This was scientifically conceived
although it puzzled the rest of the populace. More-Than-
One-Of-Us shared his/her world and when he/she lifted
a hand, we all followed suit or bowed in recognition.
We travelled together. We were always together in a restaurant.
We didn't pay taxes. We woke with one mind and heart. We
stuck together. We were not incomplete. More-Than-One-Of-
Us stayed home, we waited by the door. When he/she wished
one thing we all wished it. We caused the destruction
of Detroit by wishing this way and then we sought about
rebuilding. Sought about terminology. Courage returns.
Sought about the spirit of primitive age. Splendour of
nobility dazzles us but the court is an abyss of sins,
gate of hell, so enough of that. Sought about it about
a decade. We caused no heartbreak. We whispered a good
idea in unison. We magnetized floods and famine.
We swept out all the debris to the Plain of Good Hope.
We dumped our fears in the Canals of Forgetfulness. We
stored our memories in the Dell of Resolve. We named
our park William Shakespeare. We named the river Dante.
Sappho Avenue skirted the park. We wrote a constitution
one starry night. More-Than-One-Of-Us
scratched his/her name like a true prince/princess
at the bottom of the mile-long scroll. Let there be beautiful
forms always we said! We began transmitting to other
solar systems with the impulses of the dance. We all
died at once and became stars in a constellation that
resembled a bridge.

Thinking Right Inside The Thing

Sadness about the coaches   Jane always likes a dinner there
    She travels not so far   Yellow grass sways this way,
that, by wind   Clever to build a window there.
Concerned & wracked by ephemera of the day Jane
    flaunts her popularity   Someone's impressed, delivers
controls & frees her hand   "The perfect handle, sir."
She exudes through toxic pores lusts conceived in the brain
    She saves her syntax for a little town in Indiana
remembering how she & Jimmy dressed for dinner
"We both came up this way together   don't laud my past
    over me, no more you'll vex this lady."

Amtrak Meditation

fleeting Hudson, fleeting crimping river
fleeting lighthouse, shaky waves
rocky coast, fleeting heart
fleeting forlorn train whistle
fleeting construction, fleeting construction boss's lunch
fleeting yellow crane lifts logs
floating foliage, faint splashes of red orange chartreuse
no "no trespassing"
no "no dumping"
fleeting high flying cables
fleeting handsome red buoy & yacht—the governor's?
fleeting black man in blue & orange silk tie yawning
　　reading *The New York Times*
large blue & orange kegs roll by quickly
fleeting dayglo hardhats
fast longing
fleeting clumps of tangled green
fleeting prehistoric ferns
fleeting stalled white truck at steel bridge
fleeting smart brick mansion on gentle hill disappearing
sky-blue leatherette upholstery, fleeting
fleeting torn Beirut
smeared newsprint, fleeting
autumnal equinox, fleeting
perishing phenomena wheeling by
disappearing rail ties
point to phantom city, all out

Photos At The Edges

I was stepping out of being a teenager
I used to be ambidextrous but now energy
        flows out of you, The Gladiator
It's the hand I hold my pen in,
A little reminder of Hopis in Phoenix, but first
        Harlem summer 1953, 16, first job, 19th & 4th Ave
Rising from packer to order picker
Say "Thank you" in a dream under trees
        says Quentin R. Hand who spends the rest
        of the time reading
Next it's May where I'm older in Windsor, Ontario
If you only knew what a place attracts
If you only knew, dear misfit, how a woman's wrist
        can be silvery, old, Russian
I feel like that's me on a Monarch speed bicycle
And then it feels like what I was: percussive
Rocks on a woodblock, muted sound
Rock which is a middle sound, mute teenager
I'm stingy too, which reminds me of Equadorian
        fertility icons
They always start a lot of conversation
Now my home is near an arroyo
Skullish, it looks like what I was when I was back then

Her Night

Out of an eye comes research
Her night: portrait & a description
A night of knowledge: it was plainly hers
Two ways of writing explain this
There was her night
And then there was her night, a repetition
A night in a quarry in Helena was not anticipated
Or at dusk, before the night had started: The Lavender
     Open Pit Copper Mine near Bizbee
Everywhere she claims it as hers: purple, dark, starry
Buffalo: spring snow
Amherst: Emily Dickinson's night: what was that?
Night is anyone's guess
Naming the planets: Saturn still extant
        after all this time
And so I went on with an idea of the night
Djuna's night
All-American nights
Recesses one has one's program for
My streets are not her streets at night
Night: just like that
She dreamed her clothes were like Spanish ice-cream
She dreamed a moth came and emptied her soul to her
It was a female moth
The mosquitoes protested (they were female too)
She had the desire to include a shawl & kleenex
She walked where there'd never been a mountain
   (Can you be sure?)
She would think about walking to Sanitas Mountain at night
If any place or thought about night is left out she's sorry
For she can't even begin to remember the rooms:
     El Rito, Bellevue, the old man's stuffy sitting room
She was lost in the abstraction of the girl's perfume
Nights in front of a shrine prostrating to her potentially
     luminous mind
Sleeping late
Literature is being written at night
The couchette rattles into Trieste
A plane jets across the continent
Now I'm above the clouds & the moon is up with me
Seeing what someone else means by night is another option
She suspends all preconceptions
And forgets the concept "moon"
It could be frightening if you were a prisoner
Or, a relief
Her night is of no importance really

But there's never another one like it
Moonlight: I hear the amorous cats
Moonlight: the South American map lies on the hammock
        exposed to the elements
She did not "drop by" at 1 a.m. as supposed
But made another night call
A bird called
Confused by jet lag, time went out of her control
She shrugged & went to a party
Her escort parked the car near Coit Tower
In between lovers
Between lovers
Between textures: silk, velvet, cool cotton
Throw back the bedspread!
Out of the eye comes the moon
Out of the eye: seduction
What does it really matter what anyone does
Minnesota is just like that
She wouldn't give out her address in Oregon
Her coat was made for a night like this
Her night: where was it leading?
None knew
Display her zeal hour by hour
Opium would change this dream
Her nervousness was a blind
Talk about something like: "We in this period
        have not lived in remembering"
My excitement is my open eyes
Her clothing is of a daily-island-life variety
A line distinguishes it
She almost travelled to Tent City out of love & honor
Everything will have to be repeated in the morning
Listen: hum of typewriter, Jacqueline's loud refrigerator
        & clock
Listen: a long line of thoughts bargaining to enter in
One thought: the time is 3:15 a.m.
Another thought: there is only one way to phone her
And another: night is long to her & short to us
Not at all
Say that again
Not at all
She is ahead of herself but behind every action
Concentration was like having the night inside her
        all the time, she said
She said she'd go to any length to stay awake, imbibing
        controlled substances as well as caffeine
She said this because she was excited about making double time
This is an ordinary great deal to know

This Object

"An object looks old but is as new as a
child's tea set under cellophane
Open it now
It might be from the 30's being
fragile although nothing tangible
remains from that period in my life
This tea set with its tops and ladles
makes me happy
There were 60 pieces in all
and the one I have in my hands
is the only one that doesn't have flowers
I grew up in Wheeling, West Virginia
This object deals with my childhood
not accessible to me as I write,
inaccessible to you now, but as I write
this way to say how I ignored many other
old things which are like children now
in all my contemporary dreams, all
my empty nest dreams. This is what
the world would look like if I
were that child: smooth & functional
I'll put this box away now in the dresser
How do you say hello
when do you say goodbye"

One On Her Side

What she does with leaf, twig, bird, lorgnette
apparently strange to us is like
society parting a person from her napkin
I would go back to Chattanooga
leave the average reader to his or her *Vogue*
It'll crumble in the hand, useless
in the mountain home
It'll part the person from her nature
They say she is a plaything to fashion –
sometimes sad, smart as a whip,
funny in her way.

First Poem

I put these words down to touch them
I pull you to me, touching
I put you right next to me thinking
I caught your name. But what is it?
"Laughing Girl"
We call this "twilight"
We call this "dawn"
Where Moon go?
I sleep in the air
Food grows, I know this
I am not alone in my thinking
Now I want to make an object
so you will know my hands are alive
A Dakota spirit takes care of me
I'll mention her in a way
so you'll know her
Laughing babies come out of her belly
She's the big one with the open mouth
Her eyes are closed so she can be inside herself
She moves around freely
She comes out of her own mouth singing
like the mockingbird

Diamond

Flourite showing octagonal cleavage
from Cave-in-Rock, Harding, Illinois
invites you hither,
appears upon the scene
like a bolt of lightning,
material as nothing manmade could be
Could something manmade talk or agree?
Human palms bend toward the ineffable gypsy
whose crystal cube is struck with a glaring blow
by rude hands
The corners of the cube fall
off along weak atomic lines
leaving a diamond shaped octahedron
from which all pictures of war have been removed
replaced by anything the heart desires
Cross my palm with silver for this vivid scene.

Girl Enticed To The Sky

She lived up there. It had been her home after a
spell she was under from a Porcupine who made her
his wife. She went up a tree to the sky with him.
When alone she'd found a hole that looked down on
green. She covered it up when the others (her
in-laws) came, but later she lowered herself down on
a lariat attached to her digging stick. Her husband
found her hanging thus and hit her with a stone which
landed her on the ground. It was this way the women
returned to Vermont. The old men talked of it. Yup
yup yup they said, you can walk down any road and
see such a thing

Divination

Blurting a message in rocks, in birds
My heart met itself
& threw itself in the ocean

Now I treasure my rock-salt heart

I wore a funny hat in a foreign place
Absence of rain went on & on
Then I threw some terrible money
back to the ocean

I used to be an
Always-Walk-Quickly-To-Get-Somewhere addict
There's a music box about this which
Resembles water-damaged wallpaper
In my boy's grandmother's house

I'd fly there like silver on turquoise wings
To where details could be alleviated
By crisp, clean — was it Massachusetts? — air.

Sparrow

recognizing a life
humming, charming girl
(drops asleep)
jumping off a house-top
snowing again, the roofs
quarreling
I am old sparrow

as if sleeping made them quicker
reading a good book
(sips water) (gives money)
thanking you feelingly
charming young persons
singing O-ho
I am young sparrow

listening to world's delirium
questioning all who pass by
animals romp in the yard
walking, stopping at the gate
drinking from meandering creek
(laughs) (bird flutters)
I am, singing, the old sparrow

tiring out the wandering of her
I was young sparrow
looking back the wandering of her
I am, sadly, old sparrow
sing: old sparrow
(leads away) old sparrow

Amber's Sad Walking Song

I tried to pin my hair down
It lifted like the wind
I tried to keep my mouth shut
It ope'd, a terrible grin

Mither, I cried my belly's full of life
O Mither I'm full of him
My world is sick, he tricked me
Father: never come again

I'm walking to the edge of an inky pool
I'm tempted to jump in
Daddy's heart is black & cruel
O Mither I can't yet swim

The water could be a blanket
to hide my terrible flesh
I'll lie by the edge of the Ohio
& take the sweetest rest

Vowels

after Rimbaud

Hefty "A" you hold the world like Atlas
Will you also be a roof for the lazy animals?
Exotic "E", strangers store Egyptian treasures
     on your roomy shelves
How long will your compassion last?
Noble "I" your anorexia is shocking! Quit it!
Where have you been sleeping these dark cool nights?
"U" sits under the heavens to catch stars
Occasionally the moon drops down into her arms
A wren flies into the secret treacherous net
A woman with much hand & wrist jewelry
blows a perfect smoke ring into a spacious
     room in Cape Hatteras where friends have gathered
To watch a space shuttle lift off on TV

American Manners

You see the workers bore into the rock with a pneumatic drill.
Sometimes it is too hard for their points and they blow it
to bits with dynamite. From limestone to granite. These are
the givens while one is standing or sitting. A disquieting
smile. A long day in the Seattle sun. I find myself an
expense to my nation, coming & going. While I blunder she
(the other one, my dark sister, my double) is over the fence.
Who will keep my bridge with me? She is the beginning of my
being outside so often. Do you know what I mean? It is all
in the way I organized my house. No rooms give way to other
rooms. She spans an enormous gulf for me. Margins, mistakes . . .
O my modern friend and her negotiations! I live in the water
of her eyes. An old story of draperies, bright collections
of all you'd wish in one place to be gleaming in artificial
light (glass tubes, bottle, paperweights). Or she's like the
telephone cord, looped back through a doorway which you enter
giving on to a long corridor. I want her secret of being
out-of-doors. I gain on her inch by inch. I discomfort her
when she asks for mirth, although she laughs back. Even when
she believed herself to be alone I watched her face a wall as if
in prayer. She has a white drawn face when she isn't loved.
She has a colloquial face. She dances away from our society
and the tasks surrounding it. I tell her I now have branches
to shade her from the sun, little votive offerings I'll make
to her purity. This is a dark work of longing for her. I
tell you I saw nothing. I heard nothing. I knew something.
These are the American manners of this time from which we
both date, she and I in our nostalgic yearning for other
countries: Utopian rooms and drams.

In The Park Of Brotherly Love

Perhaps the sky was clouding over after all, the
Heavens looked forbidding
In the park the breeze was wistful
Looks like everything will be spoiled, heck!
All the wasted fuss & bustle
Depressed some of the adults, although Tom was an
Exception and stretched his long legs out from the bench
Like he was ready to settle in for the annual Rotary
Picnic anyway however long it might take—tomorrow, next week
                                    Someone cried
Hallelujah! as the napkins & paper plates took off & the pages of *The
Inquirer* unhinged & flew like big flapping birds in
A westerly direction
                    The storm is here! The storm is here!

Warbler

In being musical you put in the Jerusalem artichoke, a kind
        of sun flower, with a tuber that is cooked as a
        vegetable
You put in an artesian well
You put in glad you are fruitful, you are saturated with new
        life
Put in the impressionability of youth, haunted by lines of
        poetry—"L'amor che m'inchina" (the love that bends
        me) or "Felicitous phenomenon!"
Put in may your tongue give thanks with heroic couplets
Put in a passacaglia
In being musical you are on the verge of dancing, you take on
        the qualities of contrast in lighting and color, you
        are humming, you are no longer moderate and avoiding
        their eyes
In being musical you are naturally mnemonic
Everything is blended, all thoughts too, but you can be distinct
        if you have to, being sharp and excellent of diction
You intuitively understand mitosis in which the nuclear chromatin
        is formed into a long thread which in turn breaks into
        segments that are split lengthwise
You have been that thread
You have been those segments too
You are provided with implements like a medicine man, and the
        herbs are cooking under your nose
You beat a drum for 24 hours
Much seems imponderable but you sit in one spot nevertheless
Your mind is implicated in all this, and snow
It is winter and mounds of ice obscure your view
You see all you have imported to this place, a small cabin,
A Bulgarian chorus sings "Come To Supper Tonight, Rada". It
        is a song of the Rhodopes mountains, where mythology
        located the home of Orpheus. The Rhodope mountaineers
        are lyrical, their dialect almost Slavic with its
        gentle inflections. The theme is that in spite of
        terrible gossip, the young man will return

You fall in love with Slavic eyes
You take an item out of a large carton: a heavy brown wool
          pancho from Equador. You watched the tailor make a
          collar for it. It has twin flesh stripes, and many other
          thinner ones of night-sky blue. Something else a
          departing lover gave you sticks in your throat
In being musical you make a refrain that goes: earth air fire
          kisses and the rest
You put in a northwesterly wind and the jetstream which dips
          into your valley. Sometimes the sound of this fast
          wind is so high-pitched you think you are hearing
          coyotes
The coyotes make a yipping mantra on the night of the moon
          (I can mimic this in person)
You are nostalgic for musical ornaments, you have heard of the
          "roulade" which is a rapid succession of notes sung
          to one syllable
You remember the trade winds blowing towards the equator
You become well again, undismayed
But you are still a pagan
In an electron tube the "heater" is the element set inside the
          cathode and heated by an electric current so that it
          indirectly heats the cathode to the temperature at
          which it will give off electrons
You are warmed by little informations that sing to you
You become more and more mollescent
"Rallentando" is indicated in the piano score
Not to say you are losing muscle, your heart is thumping with
          enthusiasm
You play for generals, politicians, monarchies
You play from a mountaintop, and from a valley of low shrubbery
You can make sounds approximating the Mesozoic by beating on
          special rocks
In the cliff dwellings of Mesa Verde you are almost at home
You climb a ladder to get out of the rain
Drops of rain plunk on the tin roof
Jean Philippe Rameau is a manic composer. I am typing
The ninth month of the Moslem year, Ramadan, comes and goes
          unobserved in this little prairie town
In being musical you acquire a plectrum
The Ring Ouzel makes a pretty sound
Macgillivray's Warbler prefers moist hillside thickets

Doug's Natal Day

"Stand stiff if you'd not be undone."

—Marianne Moore

Blinders on as a condition
of getting through gauntish corridors
doesn't let us off easy
but presents to the mind certain states
like settling all preliminaries
such as this bright sun on your birthday

It exists. You too
I wish you well whatever you do

Fusionless I walk Palo Alto streets with poets' names
shadow of a euphoric Coleridge leaps out on sidewalk
in my terse brain as if to say Boo!
Cool trees, lonesome days

No, America is not *that* greenish
although we be green like envy
green like stew, like salad green,
green of glass, or grass push through
You rock like a magic man out of your cradle
to be born
abjuring magic
abjuring vanity
to be a dancer in you

Looking Down The Beautiful Pemigewasset Valley
From The Rim Trail On Cannon Mountain

Once spare of feasting eyes
a valley rests
under gaze of them

Once it was "hunter green"

Light is caught
in every pouch
Eyes remember
how forgotten
some things are

Bathers chirp in Echo Lake
A yellow cable car
sways in the sky
A child presses his nose
against the glass
Tiny shadow people walk the rim
how did we get here
ooooooo   Ahhhhhh

Ode To My Paycheck

For my poor paycheck & to my sad paycheck – amends!
Deep nets & deep pockets for my paycheck
Mediterranean bees for my paycheck
3 robust laughs to my paycheck
Russian brooms beckon my paycheck
They are held by Russian witches who curse America
Who knows the mayhem of paycheck?
Who knows fantasy & horror of paycheck?
Paychecks are not erect nor are they dirty
Maybe skillful crowbar helps you to money
Thief! Get a paycheck
Bam! Goes paycheck
I love a night of paychecks & not all go for poker
I don't want a slot machine
It's berserk how you pay for paycheck
It's never a hill of beans
Cruel taxing winds blow paycheck away
O boss give me big paycheck you've got the lettuce the cash
You make the rockets run
I'm lost in hock while Chicago Midland waits with interest
in shadow, arms like vaults, open

To Hummingbird

Odd paradigm of speed!
Ordinary galactic universe
produces tiny wing gyration
How nervous inside
yet chatty for what is combative
in the sense you combat
the air, little prince,
you do

Like wish, like thought
to rise up quickly
to disappear
Are you toy? True bird?
Or some arcane wizard?

I watch you dive
into pink flower slipper
Wyoming sunset nectar
incarnadine

The Figures

The figures had some kind of net they hoisted between them
It was buzzing
The buzz words were "gorgeous"   "glutinous"
        "ramification"   "sublets   "New Deal"
                "croneyism" & "*au pair* girl"

They had never heard "money store"
They had never visited a "condo"
nor purchased "ektachrome"

Their private ladder of words went on
Stevie climbed to the top thinking: "pith"
        "frostbite"   "exercise caution" etc.
then remembered the friend below
his opium den, his exotic pipe tobacco, Bristol Cream,
his khaki tent near the border

They were far from the amenities
Far from souvenirs and tantalizing cocktail waitresses
with their prickly little *hors d'oeuvres*

Personal Universe

wicket   Chatres   lava

oxblood   porous   campfire

monkeychant   willow   whippoorwill

bicycle   vespid   laugh

lion   dulcimer   grandfather clock

whoa   delphinium   vine

twitter   linden   Portugese

pianissimo   coltsfoot   spinach

cardamon   bannock   goatsmilk

pina   hibachi   parachute pants

clarinet   aguardiente   adobe

treacle   seaweed   semen

DMT   shakuhachi   velveteen

cactus   tension   febrile

tan   beagle   tinsel

ivory   chaise longue   leapfrog

handrail   wire   bosom

terrazo   enceinte   slate

sidewalk   formaldehyde   gardenia

cattail   fence   tapdance

trampoline   sit   balance

weave   smoke   lynx

adultery   squall   Jupiter

twilight   highhanded   orchid

tympanum   fleur de lis   heron

crescent   Gloucester   canister

versant   eyeglass   lattice

Cheops   hops   match

spice   medoc   ribbon

ink   linen   Nile

wool   tundra   Seine

lemon   atom   jade

lake   canyon   rival

Walk Around Time

Girl bouncing red ball corner Sullivan & Spring Streets 1953
makes Spanish stucco so vivid so much paint everywhere Senior High
"I've always loved things like that"
Car up in the air, Grand Prix next?
Young men fingering tires & talking shop
"You have no instruction to use that Ed Sanders"
on by the wood shop and 3-ton truck
Yellow bleachers behind a green parka & endless cars with
students in motion
Government 6614 Nebraska "That's the coach's. I'll
introduce you as Oscar Robertson's buddy"
M's story "Monroe Wheeler At The Pumps" to mind
Smell of hot body shop, heh Cinderella!
Applied Math, Consumer Math & Algebra 1–2
taught by Miss Harms, Miss Carmen, Nelson Rockefeller
and Dave Van Ronk   Pink & yellow splotches
meet a corner above mounds of dirty ice
just like we have in New York City
now if I were a groundhog. . . . . . I ain't
"Make gin outta those berries" Jack Collom says
pointing to juniper, hot house & mescal
from those cactus? geraniums in milk and remember
San Francisco's speckled leaves
Juniper like a flattop
cameos, Calculus Recourse, "Have to start kicking amen, man!"
a box springs & a faggot of wood for Magnolia Road
Christmas, Reed's poem with a "mum" in it
It is spring but
NO BEVERAGES IN THE GYM flagrant purple queer teeshirts
& a man speaking karate with an Asian accent
Video camera, kid waving scissors, containerized service
light through carnelian curtains in long ago empty room
light shifting slowly across wood
no one there the lone & level desks
sands of Nebraska raising arms to stretch

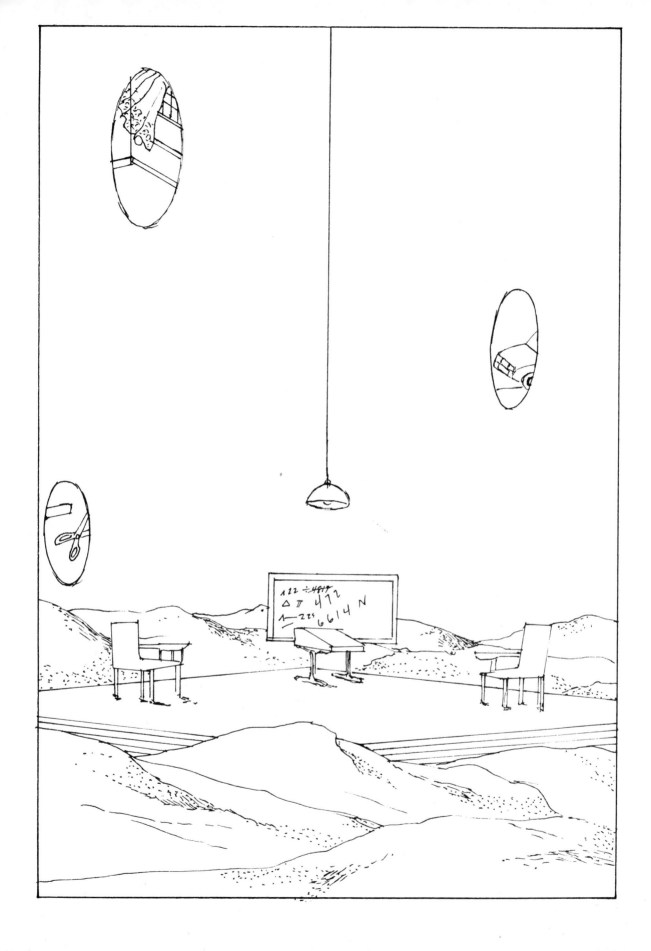

Parted Together

Missoula, I slept inside your walls
Montana, the moon is beautiful wherever you are
Montana, my girl: the mountains, the sky!
The sky exists to be nudged by mountains
Mountains look down on my narrow hands & feet
What is it to be proud like a monument?
A vested interest is picturesque
Did you know you were often rugged like this Missoula?
Animals live at your fringes
My girl you were always a haven
Business is getting on sharp as a jack knife
Business means more tall talk
Struggles between people are frequently invisible
A family seizes an opportunity
Another chance will come along I'm sure of it
My lover & I parted here once & for all
But we were violators
Girl Missoula I slept inside his boy arms inside you
One last time
I know what I'm saying: the sky, the mountains
Montana: the struggles
We parted together from here where my eyes took off
How beautiful you were
My tiny plane took off from your good looks

El Rito

Joyful, as if you neared world's end
Then sadness, a worldly smile,
as if trifling delays
are multiplied by fast youth. Biding time
as mice in a lion's den are safe from the panther
although perfectly covered by manzanita, by mesas,
by a pellet of shot, or great enchantment
It lulls and soothes me in my days
and ancient desolation, or occasionally
speaking-of-change days: a queer squawk
Yuccas spearing the wind tell us
the grey lags are coming!
I wonder at chamisa, yellow at the top
I wonder at haste, at busy ambassadors off to tell
what they see out West: centipedes, bats, rattlers,
baskets, shards, santo de ninos, exchanges, studio
light, a religious tableau depicting
the beginning and cnding of time
Go there in the full moon (somewhere else the snipe
go to the peat and heather when the moon is full)
I have a duty to adobe and to the moon. Short
evening wears off. I can't tell you what it is
As one shines in memory, another fades, and
spirits go out of the earth and into the sky at sunset
Have you seen O holy buttes?
Pinks that travel to the sky as mesa goes black,
night coming? Arroyos run like quickening of desire
A hand does not effectively contribute to the landscape
Wrinkles and dying, the ways of a dangerous world. . .
Time is sleepy here. I'm irked by nothing, but
my own boding. I'll sharpen my desert implements
Water is an issue here — precious, inestimable
Any life remaining to watch stars or dawn on this planet
knows this, standing pale amidst so much color.

Door Car Pad Hair Davids

(A Dream)

Headstrong people butt the door. Orono. But the door
won't open. They keep trying. A Mister Lando arrives,
untenable in pinstripes, but . . . But the door doesn't open
on his face either. About his face: sallow under flourescence
but intriguing, I saw it in an art gallery once: a famous
painter's great early works, modest and sleek on the white
walls, Lando's face jutting out no stranger than art really
when it paints a smile, 2 blue eyes, a streak of grey in
someone's hair. But Lando was oblique. He fingered a book.
His companion turned her head and her straight cropped
red hair danced like a curtain. They were gone. I had
a door like this one (above) once although a card ran
under it, a white one, carrying messages to the heating pad,
ionizer, bionaire, and necessary humidifier. It was a
cord. A rod ran through her hair. The print on the card
read as shown "25 Bolsitas Filtrantes Fabrica: Huayruro
Pata No. 921" in black letters against a yellow background.
The box was old, ripped, a memento of a trip to Peru. The coca
leaf teabags have a small picture of Machu Picchu printed on
them. I lift a rock and the grubs march
into the light in Orono. A wrapped something (a vessel of
Opaquing Fluid) was tied to a turtle's back. It was shady
beside the door (we'd given up trying to get inside the
Joke Store). The 2 Davids (Berrigan and Byrne) arrived
bringing hot drinks & one Count Basie oversize radio disc.
According to the script I think I was thinking this all
happened and was written before the events in El Salvador.
The taller David said "If you won't think this, who will?
Oh Ron Oh (The President) won't." He reminded me that certain
structures on the inner surface of the underside of the temporal
lobe are necessary to long-term retention of memory.
"Raymond Roussel had them, Proust, Frances Yates."

Youth & Woman

You were the talk of all my travel days
                 Mr. Teen Arrogance

You made men balmy
with your sleek shoulders on beds of Delaware
O laddie!

Don't desire me, you said
because it's sharper
how men will adore me
slipping in beside
an inclination
to be their slave

Labor Day

slouched like
a bent one
or animal
had been standing
up before
& strong
nostalgia for rain
childhood
screen door bangs
near a lake
Millville, New Jersey
end of summer
someone calls
"Annie" through
dusk
mosquitoes brush
past
decades later
say
"sit up"
jolt up
memory up
with reflected
light
starts here

Apache Tears

My heart is breaking
A-e-ya!
My heart is breaking
A-e-ya!
My heart like my father's before me
breaks — A-e-ya A-e-ya
My heart like my mother's before me
breaks
O break heart, A-e-ya

My sister cries
A-e-ya!
My brothers cry
A-e-ya A-e-ya!
Hidden in the earth
grandmother's tears
A-e-ya A-e-ya
My grandfather's tears
are watering the ground
A-e-ya A-e-ya

My heart is breaking
A-e-ya
Day breaking
A-e-ya
Ghost arrows in my heart
A-e-ya A-e-ya
O break heart, A-e-ya

Held Together With A Desk

What makes a man move?
Why do people woo & marry?
To you, who made of my young days
passion, paradox, complexity
to you, who makes me write this
I ask What's history?
Can we resolve it into a
series of pictures?
one: taboo
two: a boy with a sister
three: he who looked at the world
        through his heart
four: words became tangible
five: trips in a car
six: domestic conversation
    with a giant
seven: didn't go to cracked heaven, stayed
    on this wild earth
eight: somnambulist
nine: colors
ten: strange eyes
eleven: he raves
twelve: sheds tears
thirteen: society appears & baffles
    an "attitude"
fourteen: slender?
fifteen: terrific force of atmosphere
sixteen: there had always been baseball
seventeen: the world in your mouth, talking
eighteen: intensely breathing
nineteen: unfolding sex
twenty: a busride in Mexico
twenty-one: gentleman

twenty-two: glamourous man
twenty-three: held together with a desk
twenty-four: ruled by Mars
twenty-five: process of creation still
      incomplete
twenty-six: reverberations, interruptions
twenty-seven: more travel
twenty-eight: burning with fire of manhood's
      prime energy
twenty-nine: contented kingdom
thirty: axis shifting
thirty-one: fatherhood
thirty-two: many books
thirty-three: country living
thirty-four: looks back with a sigh
thirty-five: labors in the perfection
      of his art
thirty-six: persistent solipsism of
      the poet
thirty-seven: haircut
thirty-eight: deeper scrutiny

Scholar

Scholar bends with insurmountable problem
drifting out of small circle into humaner air
She's a moody world
but there's allurement of nourishment among amenities
Someone else's kitchen in Lexington
Ardor? Like a whip,
like glimmers of dissatisfaction
creeping in slowly with a zest
you accord passion with
making her personal pronoun personal
& wrenching of ties to her book
It is an eloquent conclusion
under the motive of nothing but sleep.

ANNE WALDMAN

Author of

GIANT NIGHT, Corinth Books, 1970
BABY BREAKDOWN, Bobbs-Merrill, 1970
NO HASSLES, Kulchur Foundation, 1971
LIFE NOTES, Bobbs-Merrill, 1973
FAST SPEAKING WOMAN, City Lights 1975 & 1978
JOURNALS & DREAMS, Stonehill, 1976
SUN THE BLOND OUT, Arif, 1976
SHAMAN, Munich Editions, 1978
COUNTRIES, Toothpaste Press 1981
CABIN, Z Press, 1981 & 1984
FIRST BABY POEMS, Rocky Ledge 1982/Hyacinth Girls 1983
MAKEUP ON EMPTY SPACE, Toothpaste Press 1984
BLUE MOSQUE, United Artists 1985

Editor of

THE WORLD ANTHOLOGY, Bobbs-Merrill, 1969
ANOTHER WORLD, Bobbs-Merrill, 1972
TALKING POETICS, Vols. I & II, Shambhala, 1978
HOMAGE TO TED BERRIGAN, Coffee House Press, 1985

SUSAN HALL

One Person Exhibitions

1972   Whitney Museum of American Art, New York, N.Y.
1975   Nancy Hoffman Gallery, New York, N.Y.
1978   Hamilton Gallery, New York, N.Y.
1981   Dart Gallery, Chicago, Illinois
1984   Neil G. Ovsey Gallery, Los Angeles, California

Selected Group Exhibitions

1973   "Extraordinary Realities", Whitney Museum of American Art
1974   "Aspects of the Figure", Cleveland Museum of Art
1977-8 Group Shows, Willard Gallery, Holly Solomon Gallery, N.Y.C.
1979   "The Decade In Review", Whitney Museum of American Art
1983   "Back to the U.S.A.", Kunstmuseum Luzern, Rheinisches
          Landesmuseum Bonn, Wurttembergischer Kunstverein Stuttgart

Public Collections

New Museum, New York, N.Y.
Hudson River Museum, Yonkers, New York
Whitney Museum of American Art, New York, N.Y.
San Francisco Museum of Art, San Francisco, California